Pitch To Publish

How to Take Your

Comic from Sketch to Shelf

Written By: Steven Nesbitt

Edited By: Jordan Franklin & Marcella Geddis

Simple But Complex, LLC

Pitch to Publish: How to Take Your Comic from Sketch to Shelf

ISBN: 979-8-218-93857-4

This publication is intended to provide accurate and authoritative information on the subject matter covered. It is sold with the understanding that the author and publisher are not providing legal, financial, accounting, or other professional services. While every effort has been made to ensure the accuracy of the information contained in this book, the author and publisher make no representations or warranties regarding its completeness or suitability for any particular purpose. They specifically disclaim any implied warranties of merchantability or fitness for a particular purpose.

The strategies and advice in this book may not be appropriate for every situation. You should consult a qualified professional when necessary. Neither the author nor the publisher shall be liable for any loss of profit or other commercial damages, including but not limited to special, incidental, consequential, or other damages.

Affiliate Disclosure: This book includes referral links to products and services I personally use and trust. If you choose to make a purchase through these links, I may earn a small commission at no additional cost to you. Your support helps me continue creating free resources, tools, and guides for creators. Thank you for being part of this journey.

Table Of Contents

Introduction

Hi there,

If you're reading this, chances are you've looked at a comic book, manga, or graphic novel and thought: *"Man, I wish I could make something like that."* Maybe you've already taken a few steps and started sketching. Maybe you've hit a wall and feel stuck. Or maybe you've just been sitting on an idea, waiting for the right moment to begin. Wherever you are, you're in the right place.

I wrote this book because I was once exactly where you are. I had the ideas, I had the passion, but I didn't have a roadmap. I didn't know what I wanted to do or how to do it. Many of the guides and manuals out there are either too expensive or overwhelming.

That's why this guide will walk you through the process step by step, in simple terms anyone can understand. My goal is to provide you with the tools you need to get your comic book out into the world on your own terms.

By the time you finish ***Pitch to Publish,*** you won't just know "How to make a *comic.*" You'll have a clear, repeatable process for taking an idea from your head to a finished, publishable comic — whether that's digital, print, or both.

This book will be broken down into 6 chapters:

1. Starting from Scratch - How to build your idea, characters, and script.

2. Making the Book - Drawing, inking, coloring, and lettering.

3. Pre-Production & Planning - Printing logistics, trim size, ISBNs, and Metadata.

4. Funding - How to pay for your comic and manage collaborators.

5. Marketing & Launching - How to build an audience, share your progress, and prepare for launch.

6. Publishing - Turning your finished comic into something people can buy and read worldwide.

This will keep things simple and easy to refer to while you embark on your journey.

To prove this works, I'll be showing you examples from comics I've already written and published. As you progress through each chapter, you'll see how I applied these steps to my projects—and how you can apply them to yours. By the end, you'll not only understand the process, but you'll also develop the skills to repeat it again with your own ideas.

Creating a comic isn't about perfection; it's about progress. Every small step you take turns your ideas into reality instead of letting them sit in your head forever. Each page you complete is proof that your story matters, and every step forward brings you closer to holding your work in your hands.

Chapter 1 – Starting from Scratch *(The Idea)*

Sections

Beat Sheets & Outlines

Script Formatting

Software, Tools, and Hardware.

What Is a Comic Book?

Before you write a script, draw a character, or open any software, it is essential to understand what a comic book truly is. A comic book or graphic novel is a visual story told through **images, dialogue, narration, and sound effects**.

Many new creators dive straight into creating elaborate and exciting scenes without understanding the underlying structure behind them, and that's where confusion and frustration often start.

A comic is not just art, and it's not just writing. It's the combination of both working together to guide the reader through a story, one moment at a time.

To understand how comics work, you first need to know the basic building blocks:

- **Panels** — The boxes that make up individual moments.
- **Dialogue & narration** — The words characters speak and the text that guides the reader through the story.
- **Page Layout**— How panels and text are organized on the page to direct the reader's eye and create a smooth, readable flow.

Once you understand these fundamentals, you can start shaping your own story with confidence.

If you've never written a story or used a drawing program before, you're in the right place. We're starting from scratch, and the best place to begin is with a simple beat sheet that turns your idea into a clear, workable story.

Beat Sheets and Outlines

Before you start scripting or drawing, you need a simple way to organize your ideas. This is where **beat sheets** come in.

Think of it as a lightweight roadmap. With a beat sheet, you always know where the story is headed, which makes the writing process smoother and far less overwhelming. Now that you know why beat sheets matter, let's walk through what they include and how to make one that works for you.

What is a Beat Sheet?

A beat sheet is a document that outlines the essential elements of your story, breaking it down into key moments or "**beats.**"

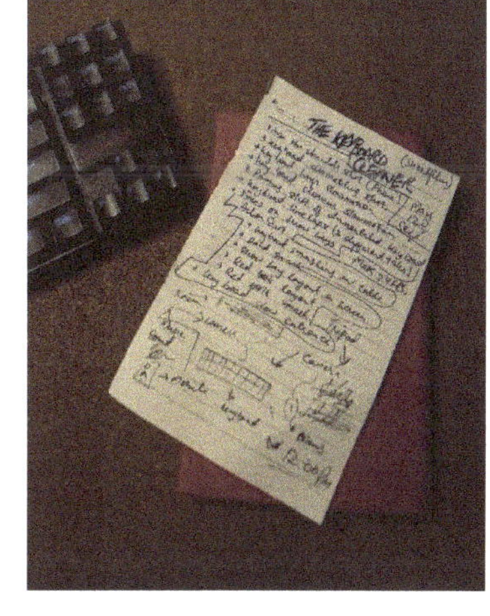

These beats represent:

- Major events
- Character decisions
- Emotional highs and lows

Unlike traditional outlines, beat sheets typically use bullet points instead of full sentences, making them concise and easy to reference during the writing process.

Before we look at examples, let's go over a few other helpful components of a standard beat sheet.

Components of a Beat Sheet

1. Characters

Who is in your story? What do they want? What stands in their way?

2. Themes

What is your story *about* at its core? Friendship? Destiny? Revenge?

3. Reference Images / Mood Boards

Visual inspiration for characters, environments, and the overall tone.

Major Beats to Include

1. Inciting Incident

The moment that disrupts the character's world and starts the story.

2. Midpoint

A major shift, reveal, or turning point that raises the stakes.

3. Climax

The big confrontation or decision that resolves the central conflict.

4. Resolution

How the story ends and what changes for the characters.

EXAMPLE BEAT SHEET (Figure 1.1)

NAME : Gems & Journeys

EXAMPLE BEAT SHEET

FILL IN THE BOXES BELOW ABOUT YOUR STORY.

STORY OVERVIEW

Finn Aiden and Malik Lief, two Journi's, set out on a quest to earn the legendary title of Huntsmen. To achieve it, they must slay a magical beast and claim its gem — the key to being granted the title.

CHARACTERS

Finn Aiden

Malik Lief

SETTING(S)

Urban Fantasy

FACTS TO SET-UP THE STORY

- ***The Huntsmen Trial:*** *A legendary rite of passage. To earn the title of Huntsman, a Journi must slay a magical beast and return with its gem.*

PLOT

BEGINNING

- Finn and Malik learn of the Huntsmen trial.

MIDDLE

- They encounter the magical beast.
- Instead of a drawn-out battle, they use traps and strategy to defeat it quickly.
- This shows their resourcefulness and teamwork rather than brute strength.

END

- They claim the gem and believe they've succeeded.
- A mysterious stranger appears and steals the gem, undermining their victory.

ELEVATOR PITCH

Gems and Journeys follows Finn Aiden and Malik Lief as they embark on a perilous quest to become Huntsmen, slay a magical beast, and claim its gem to reach the legendary land of Alamantha.

EXAMPLE BEAT SHEET (Figure 1.2)

Gems and Journeys – Beat Sheet

Chapter 0 – *Before the Beginning*

- **Legend of Ven Kward**
  - Introduces Ven Kward, the originator of the Huntsmen.
  - He forges the first Huntsmen and wields the first gem, establishing the tradition.
  - The gem is shown as both a weapon and a symbol of destiny.
- **Transition to Present Day**
  - A lone figure in a cave reads the legend, grounding the myth in modern time.
  - This creates a bridge from ancient lore to Finn and Malik's present-day journey.

Chapter 1 – *Chasing Dreams From Yesterday*

Beginning – Inciting Incident

- Finn is introduced lying in wait, preparing for his first fight.
- The Huntsmen Trial is contextualized: slay a beast, claim its gem, and earn the title.
- Finn's ambition and Malik's loyalty are established as they step into the trial.

Middle – Midpoint Confrontation

- Finn attacks the giant beast head-on.
- He uses traps to weaken and immobilize the creature, showcasing cleverness over brute force.
- Malik emerges from hiding to deliver the killing blow, cementing their teamwork.
- After victory, Finn and Malik discuss the fight, reflecting on their strengths and flaws.

Ending – Climax / Twist

- A mysterious blonde stranger has been watching them.
- He approaches, reveals cryptic secrets about their past, and offers help.
- Suspicious, Finn and Malik reject him and send him away.
- That night, by the fire, they share an emotional moment about their fight and future.
- They sleep — but awaken to find their gems stolen.
- The theft reframes their quest: it's no longer just about passing the trial, but recovering what was taken.

Writing Your Comic Script

Once your beat sheet is complete, it's time to turn your ideas into a script. A comic script is not the same as a movie script or a novel.

It is a practical document that tells the artist what to draw, what the reader will see, and how the story should flow from panel to panel.

There is no single "correct" way to format a comic script. Every creator develops their own style over time. What matters most is clarity.

Most comic scripts include these basic elements:

1. **Page Numbers** - Each page of your script should match a page in your comic. This keeps your pacing consistent and makes it easier to plan your story from start to finish.

2. **Panels per Page:** Divide each page into panels. For beginners, **4–5 panels per page** is a safe starting point.

3. **Panel Descriptions -** These shape how each scene looks and reads. Your text, dialogue, and reference images work together here to keep the vision clear, especially if someone else is drawing the comic.

Dialogue, Balloons, Captions, and Sound Effects

Dialogue and sound effects are just as important as the visuals. They bring your comic to life, guide the reader's experience, and help shape the tone of each scene.

Balloons are the shapes that hold a character's words or thoughts.

- **Speech balloons** show what a character is saying out loud.
- **Thought balloons** show what a character is thinking internally.

Captions are text boxes used for narration, scene transitions, or an internal monologue that isn't shown as a thought balloon.

Sound effects (SFX) are written sounds like *BAM*, *WHOOSH*, or *CLICK* that add energy and clarity to the action.

All dialogue, captions, and sound effects should be written directly into your script, so the artist (or you) knows exactly where they belong on the page.

How to Format Dialogue and Narration

1. Use parentheses to show who is speaking

Always place the character's name in parentheses before their spoken line. This makes it instantly clear who is talking.

- (Sam): **I can't wait to become an adventurer!**

2. Use brackets for thoughts or narration

Brackets indicate when a line is either internal (a character's thoughts) or narration (the storyteller's voice).

- [Sam]**: I hope I don't get hurt in the process.**
- [Narrator]: **As Sam approaches his destiny, his confidence begins to shake.**

3. Bold dialogue for clarity

Bold text makes dialogue and narration stand out, making it easier to review, edit, and letter your pages without missing anything important.

- (Lena): **I can't believe this is really happening!**
- [Narrator]: **As the storm gathers overhead, Lena realizes her journey has only just begun.**

EXAMPLE SCRIPT (Figure 1.3)

1

THROUGH THE RED MOON

Panel 1

Long Panel. Wide shot of hieroglyphs, that show humanity trying to climb to the moon.

[Jordi] : Ya know, my grandmother used to tell me this story about towers that went to heaven.

[Jordi] She said that before we had all these lunar shards, humanity was desperate for power to make us stronger.

Panel 2

Box Panel. A man stands on a mountain, trying to convert people to his cause. The crowd looks on in awe.

[Jordi] : So they gathered their smartest minds and built a tower that could reach the skies.

Panel 3

Box Panel. A massive tower is being erected.

[Jordi]: And after a few centuries... they actually made it to the moon.

Panel 4

Long Panel. Humans surround something shiny on the moon. It should be a striking shot.

[Jordi] That's when they found it... the first lunar shard.

Tools You Need

Before you can bring a comic to life, you need the right tools to support your creative process. The hardware and software you choose should help you stay organized, simplify your workflow, and keep your focus on the story you want to tell rather than on technical details.

In this section, we will cover the essentials: the gear that helps you draw, the programs that streamline your workflow, and the writing tools that make planning and scripting easier.

By the end, you will know not only what tools to use but why they matter. This will help you build a setup that fits your style, your budget, and your creative goals.

Drawing Tablets

You do not need expensive equipment to start making comics. Many creators begin with simple tools and upgrade later. Here are reliable options for every budget:

- **Wacom Intuos (Small)** - A basic screenless drawing tablet that is affordable, durable, and perfect for beginners who want to try digital art without a large investment.

- **XP-Pen Tablets** - Great mid-range tablets with both screen and non-screen models. They offer solid performance at a reasonable price.

- **iPad + Apple Pencil** - Portable, powerful, and excellent for drawing anywhere. It costs more, but many artists use this as their main device for full comic production.

- **Scanner or Photocopier** - If you prefer drawing on paper but want to color or edit digitally, you will need a scanner to upload your artwork into your drawing software.

Drawing Software

You can create a full comic using free programs, paid programs, or a mix of both. Choose the option that feels comfortable and fits your workflow.

Free Options

- **Krita** – A powerful, free digital painting program with layers, brushes, and high-resolution support. Many beginners use it for full comic production.
- **MediBang Paint** – Designed specifically for manga and comics. Includes panel tools, fonts, screen tones, and cloud saving. Great for manga-style storytelling.
- **FireAlpaca** – Lightweight, fast, and beginner-friendly. It has fewer advanced features but is more than enough for clean comic pages.

Paid Options

- **Clip Studio Paint (Pro/EX)** – One of the most popular tools for comics and manga. Includes paneling tools, speech bubbles, perspective rulers, and 3D models.
- **Procreate (iPad)** – A powerful and affordable app for iPad users. Great for sketching, inking, and full pages. Simple, intuitive, and fast.
- **Adobe Photoshop** – A professional standard for digital art. Very flexible but subscription-based and more complex. Best used if you're already familiar with it.

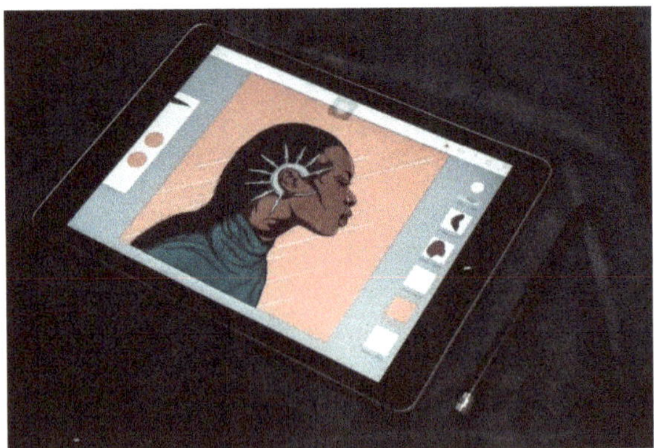

Writing & Document Tools

Even if you aren't drawing your comic yourself, you'll need tools for outlining, scripting, and organizing your ideas.

- **Google Docs** – Great for writing scripts, outlining, and collaborating with artists or editors in real time. Free, cloud-based, and accessible anywhere.
- **LibreOffice** – A solid free alternative to Microsoft Word. Ideal for offline writing and document structuring.
- **Adobe Acrobat or PDF Gear** – Useful for combining pages into PDFs and exporting final versions for publishing. PDF Gear is free and surprisingly capable.

Chapter 1 — Internal Checklist

You're ready to move on if you can say "yes" to the following:

1. ☐ I understand the core idea of my comic.
2. ☐ I can explain my story in one or two sentences.
3. ☐ I know who my main characters are and what they want.
4. ☐ I have a clear beginning, middle, and end in mind.
5. ☐ I understand what a beat sheet is and how it helps.
6. ☐ I feel confident enough to start shaping scenes or pages.
7. ☐ I know which tools I want to use for writing or sketching.

Chapter 2 – Making the Book *(The Production)*

Sections

Drawing, Inking, Coloring, & Lettering

Creating the Cover

Stages of Creation

Every comic goes through these essential stages of production. Think of them as the backbone of your workflow:

- **Drawing**: Rough sketches of characters, environments, and panel layouts.
- **Inking**: Refining linework for clarity and print-readiness.
- **Coloring/Shading**: Adding tone, mood, and depth with shadows, highlights, and effects.
- **Backgrounds**: Establishing environments that anchor the story. Even simple settings help immerse readers.
- **Lettering**: Dialogue balloons, captions, and sound effects — the "voice" of your comic.

- **Cover**: The most important piece of your book. It's the first impression that attracts readers and drives sales.

Drawing

This is where your script and reference images start to take shape on the page.

Tips for success:

- **Begin with rough sketches -** Start with loose, simple drawings to define the idea of each panel and what needs to happen in the scene.
- **Use colored pencils or pens for the first layer**: Red or blue sketch lines make it easier to distinguish drafts from final ink. When you ink over them, the sketch won't interfere.
- **Iterate with multiple drafts**: Redraw panels or pages several times. Each pass adds clarity and detail, strengthening the final product.

- **Think about flow**: When sketching, consider the reader's journey. Think about how characters move, how panels connect, where text bubbles should go, and how the eye travels across the page.

EXAMPLE IN PRACTICE (Figure 2.1)

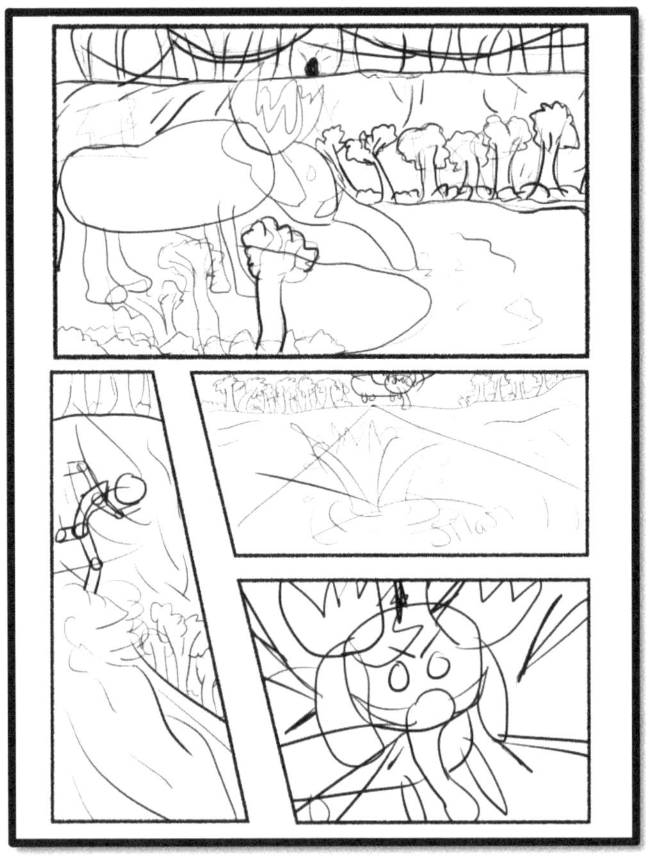

Inking

Inking is where sketches become clean, defined artwork. If you're working digitally, use separate layers for sketching, inking, and coloring.

Purpose: Define shapes, clean up messy sketches, and prepare the page for coloring.

Tips:

- **Vary line thickness to add depth and emphasis**. Thicker lines bring objects forward; thinner lines push them back.
- **Add shading or texture with repeated lines, dots, or patterns.** This suggests volume, fabric, or atmosphere even without color.

Coloring

Coloring brings your comic to life and sets the emotional tone.

Think about the mood: Choose a consistent palette. Bright colors suit energetic stories, muted tones fit serious ones, and monochromatic palettes create drama.

- **Start with "flats": Flats are simple, solid base colors** used to separate characters, objects, and backgrounds. They act as a map for the rest of the coloring process and make shading easier.
- **Add shading and highlights**: Shading adds shadows and depth, while highlights bring out light and form. You don't need to use advanced techniques here, just understanding the basics can make the scene feel more defined.

Backgrounds

Backgrounds set the stage for your characters and immerse readers in your world.

- **Draw your own**: Sketch basic settings like rooms, streets, or landscapes.
- **Download royalty-free assets**: Use free or licensed backgrounds from stock sites or comic asset packs.

Keep it simple: Backgrounds should support the story, not overwhelm it. Even minimal environments anchor the narrative.

Lettering

Lettering is where your comic finds its voice. Dialogue, narration, and sound effects merge with the art.

Best practices:

- **Balloon placement**: Position balloons to follow natural reading order (left-to-right, top-to-bottom). Each balloon should guide the eye to the next.
- **Font choice**: Use comic-specific fonts (Blambot, Comicraft) or hand-lettering for authenticity. Avoid standard word processor fonts.
- **Spacing**: Leave enough room inside balloons so text doesn't feel cramped. White space improves readability.

EXAMPLE IN PRACTICE (Figure 2.2)

Creating the Cover

Sizing basics:

- Match your comic's trim size (final cut dimensions).
- Multiply trim width by 2 (front + back).
- Add spine width (provided by your printer based on page count).
- Add bleed margins (usually 0.125" on each side).

Example: For a comic trim size of 6.63" × 10.25":

- Front + Back = 6.63" × 2 = 13.26"
- Add spine (0.25") = 13.51"
- Add bleed (0.125" each side) = 13.76" total width
- Height = 10.25" + 0.25" bleed = 10.50"

Final cover file size: **13.76" × 10.50"** for a 32-page comic at that trim size.

EXAMPLE COVER (Figure 2.3)

Chapter 2 — Creative Checklist

By the end of this chapter, I can confidently say:

1. ☐ I understand the stages of comic creation.
2. ☐ I know how drawing, inking, coloring, and lettering work together.
3. ☐ I can visualize how my pages will flow.
4. ☐ I know which tools and methods suit me best.
5. ☐ I understand how to take a page from rough sketch to final art.
6. ☐ I feel comfortable experimenting and revising through drafts.
7. ☐ I have an early idea of what my cover might look like.

Chapter 3 – Pre-production & Planning

Sections

Publishing Basics

You've planned your story, written your script, and created your pages. Now it's time to prepare your comic for the real world. We'll discuss printing, digital publishing, ISBNs, metadata, and everything else that makes your book look professional and ready for readers.

This chapter covers the essential technical details of publishing. While these aspects may not be the most exciting parts of creating a comic, they are crucial for ensuring your book prints correctly, displays properly online, and reaches readers without any issues.

By the end of this chapter, you will understand:

- Trim sizes, bleed, margins, and safe zones.
- Printing and publishing Basics
- ISBNs and their uses
- Metadata, SEO, and book tags

These details may seem intimidating at first, but once you understand them, they become simple tools that help make your comic look clean, polished, and professional.

Trim Size

This is the final dimensions of a book after it's printed, and the pages are cut or trimmed. It is expressed as width x height and measured in inches in the U.S. and in millimeters in Europe.

Common Sizes include.

- 5.5×7.5 – Standard for small comics and Mangas.
- 6×9 – Average size of most books.
- 6.63×10.25 – Typical for trade paperbacks and graphic novel size.

For example:

A standard Marvel/DC paperback is 6.63×10.25.

Why does trim size matter?

A book's trim size will impact several aspects of the final product, including page count, cover design, and possibly printing costs. The trim size you select will also affect your book's overall presentation.

How should I pick my book's trim size?

You should choose your trim size based on your personal preference and what best serves your story. Different sizes create different experiences for the reader, so pick the format that complements your art style, pacing, and overall presentation.

Bleed

Bleed is the extra space around your artwork that extends beyond the trim line. It ensures that images or backgrounds that reach the edge of the page don't get cut off during printing.

Standard Bleed

Most print-on-demand platforms (KDP, Lulu, IngramSpark) recommend a **0.125-inch bleed** on all sides.

Example:

If your trim size is **6.63 × 10.25**, your full canvas with bleed becomes:

- **6.88 × 10.50 inches**

Best Practices

- Always extend backgrounds and full-page illustrations to the bleed line.

The Safe Zone

The safe zone is the area *inside* the trim line where all important text and visuals should stay. Keeping your artwork within this space prevents dialogue, captions, or key details from being cut off during trimming or disappearing near the edges.

The Gutter

The gutter is the space where the pages meet near the spine. The **fold**, which is the curved center area where the book bends, is part of the gutter and can swallow artwork if you place it too close.

- On **single pages**, the gutter works like an **inner margin**, giving you the protected space along the inside edge of the page.

- On **double-page spreads**, the gutter becomes a major part of your layout because anything placed too close to the fold can disappear into the spine.

Why It Matters

If text, dialogue, or important artwork sits too close to the gutter or fold, it can become distorted or lost once the comic is bound. Planning for this space ensures your storytelling stays clear and readable.

Best Practices

- Avoid placing character faces, hands, or key moments near the middle.
- Plan double-page spreads carefully so nothing essential gets swallowed by the spine.

EXAMPLE TEMPLATE (FIGURE 3.1)

Publishing Options

Sections

Digital Publishing

Print-On-Demand

Global Distribution

Digital Publishing (eBooks)

Digital publishing is a low-risk way to get your comic into readers' hands. You upload your files, set your price, and your comic becomes available instantly.

Platforms include:

- Amazon KDP
- Gumroad
- Apple Books
- Your own website

No printing. No shipping. No inventory.

Digital File Standards

These are the core technical settings your comic pages must follow to display correctly on all major digital platforms.

- **Resolution: 300 DPI**
- **Color Profile: RGB**
- **File Formats:** PNG, PDF, or fixed-layout EPUB
    - **EPUB:** Required for Kindle, Apple Books, and most e-readers.
    - **PDF:** The most common format for digital comics and graphic-heavy books.

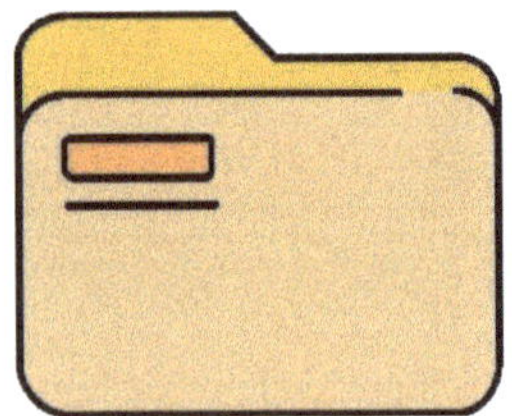

Cover File Requirements

A separate cover file is required for all digital publishing platforms.

Specifications:

- **Format: JPG or PNG**
- **Design Guidelines:** High contrast, clear typography, and fully readable at thumbnail size.

Platform Selection

Popular digital distribution channels include:

- **Amazon KDP** — The largest digital marketplace, offering global reach, built-in royalty management, and seamless integration with Kindle devices.
- **Gumroad** — Ideal for direct-to-consumer sales with simple setup and flexible pricing options.
- **Self-Hosted Website** — A self-hosted website gives you full control over your distribution, pricing, branding, and customer data. Platforms such as Shopify, WooCommerce, Squarespace, and WordPress make it easy to sell digital files without requiring advanced technical skills.

Choosing a Hosting Provider

Finding the right hosting provider can feel overwhelming, especially when you are trying to focus on creating. I have tried several options over the years, and the one that has been the most reliable for my author site is **Hostinger**.

Key features include:

- **Hosting for up to 50 websites**
- **WordPress and WooCommerce included** with no extra plugin costs
- **Fast and reliable performance** for stores, portfolios, and digital downloads
- **A simple setup** that does not require technical experience

If you're a creator who wants control without the headache, this is one of the best values you can start with

If you want the same reliable setup I use, you can scan the code or tap the link to get your discount.

You can use my referral link to get 20% off your first plan if you decide it's a good fit.

https://hostinger.com?REFERRALCODE=SimplyComplex

Physical Publishing

Physical publishing also introduces an important decision for creators: how to produce their printed copies. This is where Print-on-Demand (POD) emerges as one of the most accessible and cost-effective options.

Print-On-Demand (POD)

Print-On-Demand books are published only when an order is placed, allowing authors to avoid upfront printing costs and inventory management.

This approach eliminates the need for large print runs and reduces the financial risk associated with traditional publishing. Instead of printing hundreds or thousands of copies upfront, authors can produce as many copies as needed, making it an ideal solution for self-publishing and niche markets.

Print-On-Demand Companies

- **Amazon KDP** – Offers global reach through Amazon marketplaces, allowing your comic to be purchased worldwide. Printing is handled locally based on order location, reducing shipping times and costs. Ideal for digital-first distribution with fast fulfillment.
- **Barnes & Nobles Press** - Provides access to the Barnes & Noble retail ecosystem, enabling your comic to be sold online and potentially stocked in physical stores. They offer high-quality printing, competitive pricing, and an easy setup process, making it an excellent option for creators seeking bookstore visibility without complex distribution requirements.

- **IngramSpark** - Provides extensive bookstore and library distribution, including independent bookstores. They also offer higher-quality options and reduced printing costs when you order in larger quantities.
- **Lulu** - High-quality printing with professional-grade paper, global distribution, and integration with Shopify and WooCommerce. Costs are higher than KDP, but it's ideal for premium editions or special releases.

What is Global Distribution?

Global distribution is the system that makes your comic available to readers beyond your own storefront. Instead of you handling every sale directly, this is a setting offered by print-on-demand platforms that connects your book to a worldwide network of retailers, libraries, and online shops. Think of it as the "highway" that delivers your comic to places like Amazon, Barnes & Noble, Apple Books, and international bookstores.

Why It Matters

Global distribution means: You don't have to negotiate with each bookstore individually. Your comic can reach readers in different countries with minimal extra effort, and both print and digital formats can be listed in multiple marketplaces simultaneously.

In short: global distribution is a Print-On-Demand option that bridges your publishing platform and the worldwide audience you want to reach.

ISBNs - Your Comic's Stamp on the World.

As you move from making your comic to preparing it for the world, there are a few professional tools you'll need to understand. ISBNs are one of the simplest, and they play a bigger role than most new creators expect.

An ISBN (International Standard Book Number) is a unique identifier assigned to your book. It comes in the form of the barcode on the back of the book. Think of it like a fingerprint or passport: it tells bookstores, libraries, and distributors exactly which edition of your comic they're dealing with, and it tells the world:

- **Who published it?**
- **What version it is.**
    - (eBook, paperback, hardback all needs separate ones)
- **What country it's from.**
- **How to categorize it.**

Why ISBNs Matter

If you plan to sell physical copies of your comic in bookstores or through distributors such as IngramSpark, you will need an ISBN. This identifier makes your book truly retail-ready by enabling it to be:

- Tracked
- Cataloged
- Stocked
- Discovered in global databases

It also officially lists you (or your imprint) as the publisher of record, which is a significant step toward establishing a professional brand.

How to Obtain an ISBN

Purchase Your Own ISBN (The Professional Route)

Purchasing your own ISBN grants you full control and ownership. You are listed as the publisher of record, and you can use the same ISBN across multiple platforms for the same format.

Benefits:

- You can upload the same book to multiple platforms
- You will retain publisher credit under your brand name
- Allows you to maintain consistency across print editions

  Where to buy (U.S.): *ISBNs are sold exclusively by Bowker.*

Free ISBN (Platform-Provided)

Many platforms offer free ISBNs when you publish through them. These are valid and functional, but they come with limitations.

Platforms that offer free ISBNs:

- Amazon KDP
- Ingramspark
- Draft2Digital. (eBooks + print)
- Blurb

Drawbacks:

- The platform is listed as the publisher.
- You can't reuse the ISBN elsewhere.
- Switching platforms requires a new ISBN.
- Limits your ability to build a consistent brand.

Which Should You Choose?

Ask yourself:

- **If you care about long-term branding and control:**
    - Buy your own ISBN.
- **If you're testing the waters with your first release:**
    - Use a free ISBN.

If you're unsure, choose the option that feels most manageable right now. You can always adjust and upgrade as your publishing vision grows.

Converting Your ISBN Into a Barcode

Once you have your ISBN, the next step is to convert it into a barcode for the back cover of your book. Most self-publishing platforms will generate one automatically, but if you want full control over the design or if you are preparing your files manually, you can easily create your own.

How to Create Your Barcode

1. **Start with your ISBN.**
2. **Use a free online barcode generator.** Just search "ISBN barcode generator," or try one of these reliable options:
   - **Kindlepreneur Barcode Generator**
   - **TEC-IT Barcode Generator (barcode.tec-it.com)**
3. **Download your barcode.** Export it as a PNG or SVG for the cleanest print quality.

4. **Place it on the back cover.** Add the barcode near the bottom corner of your back cover, leaving enough margin so it won't get trimmed off during printing.

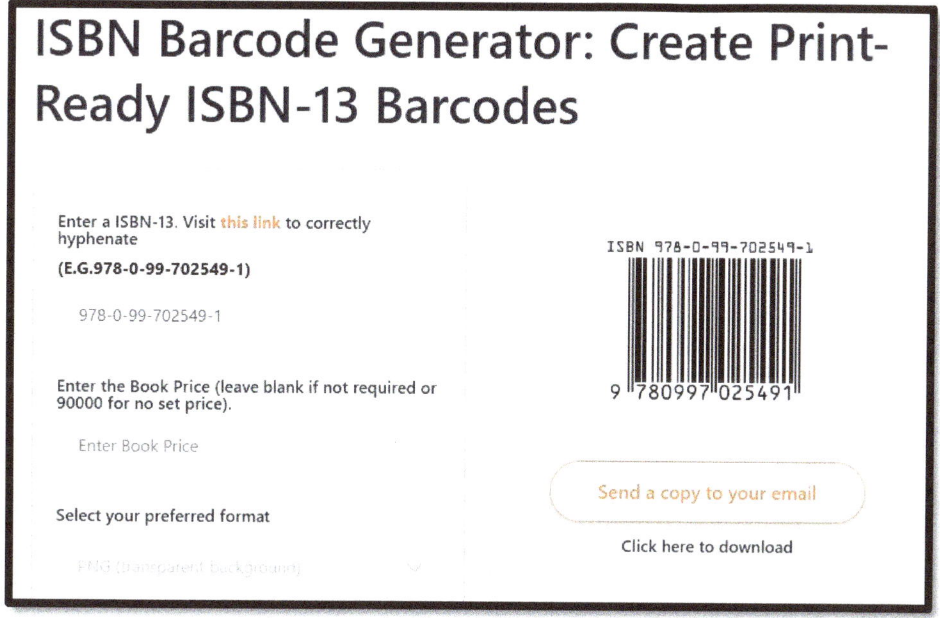

Metadata, SEO, and Book Tags

Publishing isn't just about making your comic available. It's about making sure readers can find it. That's where metadata, SEO, and book tags come in. Think of them as the invisible scaffolding that connects your comic to search engines, bookstore catalogs, and recommendation algorithms.

Metadata: The Basics

Metadata is the structured information distributors and retailers use to categorize and display your comic. Good metadata makes your book discoverable. Bad metadata makes it invisible.

Key elements:

- **Title & Subtitle**: Clear, searchable, and descriptive.
- **Author/Publisher Name**: Establishes credibility and ownership.
- **ISBN**: Unique identifier for cataloging.
- **Format & Price**: Paperback, hardcover, eBook, with a clear retail price.
- **Description/Blurb**: A concise, compelling pitch that doubles as marketing copy.

- **Categories/Genres**: Places your comic on the right shelves (e.g., *Graphic Novels > Fantasy*).

SEO: Speaking Google's Language

SEO (Search Engine Optimization) helps search engines understand what your comic is about so they can show it to the right people. When you use clear titles, strong keywords, and accurate descriptions, you're essentially "speaking Google's language." Good SEO makes it easier for readers to find your comic when they search for genres, themes, or topics related to your work. It's one of the simplest ways to increase visibility without paid advertising.

Best practices:

- **Keywords in descriptions**: Use terms your audience would type (e.g., *indie fantasy comic, self-published graphic novel*).
- **Compelling blurb**: Search engines index your description, so make it keyword-rich but natural.
- **External presence**: Blog posts, social media, and reviews linking to your comic boost visibility.

Book Tags: Your Comic's Hashtags

Tags are keywords or phrases you attach to your book in publishing platforms. They help algorithms recommend your comic to readers browsing similar titles.

Examples:

- **Genre tags**: *Superhero, Fantasy, Slice of Life*
- **Audience tags**: *Young Adult, Adult, All Ages*
- **Theme tags**: *Friendship, Adventure, Identity*

Tips:

- **Book Tags:** 7–10 strong, relevant keywords
- Avoid overly broad terms like "book" or "comic."
- Think like a reader: what would you type to find your comic?

EXAMPLE METADATA FORM (Figure 2.1)

Metadata & Categories Reference Sheet

TITLE: *Go Home, Anthony*

AUTHOR: Steven Nesbitt

PUBLISHER/IMPRINT: Simple But Complex, LLC

PRICE: $9.99

Categories (Retail/Distributor Options)

- Comics & Graphic Novels > Romance
- Comics & Graphic Novels > Coming of Age
- Comics & Graphic Novels > Fantasy & Magic *(if time travel is emphasized)*
- Literature & Fiction > Short Stories & Anthologies
- Teen & Young Adult > Romance

Book Tags (Keywords/SEO)

- Fantasy comic
- Time travel adventure *(if applicable)*
- Coming-of-age graphic novel
- Romantic quest
- Huntsmen trial
- Indie comic
- Self-published graphic novel
- Emotional storytelling
- Young adult romance
- Mythic fantasy

Chapter 3 — Technical Confidence Checklist

What you should understand before preparing your files:

1. ☐ I understand trim size, bleed, margins, and safe zones.
2. ☐ I know the difference between digital and print requirements.
3. ☐ I understand what an ISBN is and when I need one.
4. ☐ I know the basics of metadata and why it matters.
5. ☐ I feel confident choosing a publishing path that fits my goals.
6. ☐ I understand how global distribution works.

Chapter 4 - Funding Your Comic.

Sections

Outsourcing

Pre Orders & Crowdfunding

Marketing & Launch Calendar

Outsourcing

Not every creator handles every stage of comic production themselves, and that's completely normal. Outsourcing is common in the professional world because it saves time, raises quality, and allows you to focus on your strengths while still producing a polished final product.

Examples of Outsourcing

- Hiring a colorist if coloring isn't your strength.
- Commissioning a letterer for clean, professional dialogue placement
- Bringing in an editor to help refine pacing or clarity.

Outsourcing doesn't make you any less of a creator. It makes you a project lead, building a team to bring your vision to life.

Budgeting Basics

Before hiring anyone, ensure your budget is clear, realistic, and well-organized. A bit of planning upfront can prevent significant stress later.

What to Prepare

- **Contracts.** A good contract should outline deliverables, deadlines, revision limits, ownership rights, and payment schedules. This protects both you and your collaborators.
- **Estimate Costs.** Research average rates for artists, colorists, letterers, and editors. Knowing the going rate helps you avoid underpaying or overspending.

- **Prioritize Tasks.** Break your project into "must-have" and "nice-to-have" items. Essentials like art, lettering, and editing come first. Extras like variant covers or bonus prints can wait.
- **Plan Ahead.** Use a simple spreadsheet or checklist to track costs, invoices, and funding sources. Staying organized keeps your project on schedule and within budget.

What To Watch Out For

- Offers that seem too good to be true.
- Extremely low rates or promises of instant delivery.
- Unclear contracts or vague expectations
- Ghosting or inconsistent communication
- Unverified portfolios — always confirm that samples belong to the artist.

How to Protect Yourself

- Use trusted platforms that offer dispute resolution.
- Set clear expectations: deadlines, file formats, revision limits, and payment schedule.
- Request milestones or partial payments instead of paying everything upfront.
- Keep communication in writing (email or platform messages) so you have a record.

Good outsourcing is built on clarity, communication, and mutual respect. When those pieces are in place, collaboration becomes one of the most powerful tools in your creative process.

Artist-Focused Platforms

Here are reliable places to find artists and collaborators:

- **Behance** — Portfolio-driven, great for discovering professional illustrators and comic artists.
- **Fiverr** — Wide range of artists with strong comic and manga presence.
- **Upwork** — Freelance marketplace where artists often advertise commissions.

Each platform has its own strengths, so explore a few and see which one fits your workflow.

Crowdfunding

Crowdfunding is more than just raising money; it is a way to generate interest and invite readers to support your comic early in its development. Through crowdfunding, you can present your idea to a broader audience, share your progress, and raise funds to pay artists or cover production costs. Think of every pledge as someone saying, "***I believe in this project.***"

Crowdfunding Websites

Indiegogo

Indiegogo is a flexible crowdfunding platform that supports a wide range of projects, from tech gadgets and creative endeavors to social causes.

- **Funding Models**: Choose between Flexible (keep all funds raised even if you miss your goal) or Fixed (only receive funds if you meet your goal).
- **Audience**: Stronger in technology, hardware, and social impact projects, which can make finding a comic audience more challenging.
- **Ease of Use**: Onboarding is simple, and you can launch projects even in early phases.
- **Indemand**: Continue raising money after the campaign ends with no deadlines or fundraising targets.

Kickstarter

Kickstarter is the most popular platform for creative projects, including comics, films, music, and games.

- **Funding Model**: All-or-nothing. If you do not meet your goal by the deadline, no money is exchanged.
- **Requirements**: You must present something tangible, and projects are reviewed before launch.
- **Campaign Length**: Campaigns can last between 1 and 60 days. This requires careful planning but also ensures backers are intentional.
- **Audience**: Backers here are primed for creative work, making it a strong fit for comics.

Campaign Essentials

Before starting your campaign, prepare these essentials so you can launch with confidence and hit the ground running.

- **Clear Pitch.** Share why this comic matters, what makes it unique, and how backers will be part of bringing it to life. A short video or campaign page works best.
- **Visuals.** Mock-ups, sample pages, or concept art will help people see the vision.
- **Reward Tiers.**

  Keep Rewards simple and achievable

  - $5–10: Digital copy of the comic
  - $20–30: Print copy plus extras.
- **Stretch Goals.** Offer extras if funding exceeds the target. Variant covers, bonus short comics, or behind-the-scenes content keep excitement alive.

- **Timeline and Delivery Plan.** Backers want to know *when* they will receive their rewards. Share a realistic timeline for digital delivery, printing, and shipping.
- **Budget Transparency.** Show how funds will be used (printing, paying artists, shipping). Even a simple breakdown builds trust and makes backers feel confident.
- **Community Engagement.** Plan updates during the campaign. Share progress, thank backers, and keep the excitement alive. Crowdfunding is as much about building relationships as raising money.

Here are some things to think through before you launch:

- **Artist Costs**: Do your artists, letterers, or colorists charge per page? Do they add extra for coloring?
- **Payment Terms**: Will they need payment upfront, or do they accept partial payments?
- **Turnaround Time**: How long will it realistically take for the work to be finished?
- **Shipping**: How long will printing and shipping take once the comic is ready?
- **Campaign Timing**: When is the best time to launch? Do you already have enough progress to show backers?
- **Deadlines**: On Kickstarter, once you set a deadline, it's locked in. Make sure you can deliver on time.
- **Fees**: Platforms typically take 5–8% in fees plus payment processing.

Easy and Doable Rewards

Not every reward has to be complicated or expensive. Here are simple, manageable options that beginners can deliver without stress:

- **Digital Wallpapers** — Comic art resized for desktops or phones. Easy to create and send.
- **Stickers** — Print small runs of character art or logos. Affordable and fun for backers.
- **Printable Extras** — PDF posters, coloring pages, or mini art prints that backers can download and print themselves.
- **Behind-the-Scenes Content** — Share sketches, process notes, or a short making-of PDF. Adds value without extra cost.
- **Name in the Credits** — A shout-out in the comic or campaign updates. Free to deliver but meaningful for backers.

Chapter 4 — Planning & Support Checklist

What you should understand if you are planning on funding or outsourcing:

1. ☐ I understand my own strengths and where I may want help.
2. ☐ I know what outsourcing is and how to approach it safely.
3. ☐ I understand how to budget realistically for my project.
4. ☐ I know the basics of crowdfunding and what makes a strong pitch.
5. ☐ I feel confident deciding whether to hire help or work solo.
6. ☐ I understand how to protect myself when working with freelancers.

Chapter 5 - Marketing & Launching Your Comic

You don't need a massive following to build excitement around your book. What matters most is bringing people along for the ride. Hype is really just sharing the process in a way that feels natural and inviting. When people can follow your progress, they start to feel connected to it, and that connection is what makes them invested.

Pre-Orders

Pre-orders are an easy and fun way to build excitement for your comic book. They also let you raise money before committing to printing, which reduces risk and builds excitement around your project.

How to Launch Pre-Orders

Prepare your pitch.

- **Upload visuals**: Add your comic's cover, sample pages, or character art with a clear purchase button so supporters can act immediately.
- **Write a clear description**: In 2–3 sentences, explain exactly what buyers will get and when.

- **Set your pricing.**
    - Digital copies: usually sell at **$5–10** depending on length.
    - Print copies: usually sell at **$15–25**, based on page count and printing costs.

Open pre-orders.

- **Announce the launch**: Share your pre-order link on social media, in your newsletter, and within any community groups you're a part of. Use eye-catching visuals and a clear call-to-action like *"Reserve your copy today!"*
- **Set a clear window**: Keep the pre-order window open for 4–6 weeks to build momentum but short enough to create urgency.

Collect payments.

- **The money goes straight to you** — giving you the funds you need to cover printing, software, or collaboration costs.

Order Copies.

- Once you close pre-orders, use the collected funds to order author copies from your POD service (like IngramSpark, or Lulu).
- Author copies are usually cheaper than retail price, so this will maximize your margin.
    - Note: Amazon Author Copies have **"Do Not Resale"** watermarked on the book.

Deliver on time.

- Send digital copies immediately once ready.
- Ship and sign the physical copies as soon as they arrive from the printer.

Platforms to Use

- **Gumroad**: Quick setup, great for digital-first creators.
- **Shopify**: Full e-commerce platform with branding options.
- **Ko-fi**: Combines pre-orders with ongoing support.
- **Payhip**: Simple option for selling PDFs or print copies directly.

The Advantage of Pre-Orders for Your Comic

- **Early supporters love exclusivity** Your first buyers will feel like insiders who helped bring your comic to life. This builds loyalty and gives you a core audience that's invested in your journey.

- **Risk-free printing** You only produce what's already paid for. That means no wasted money on unsold stock and no guessing how many copies to print. Every book is backed by real demand.

- **Momentum builder** Announcing pre-orders creates urgency and buzz. Readers don't want to miss out, so they're more likely to commit early. This momentum can carry into your launch and beyond.

- **Proof of demand** Pre-orders show you exactly how much interest exists before you invest heavily in production. It's a low-risk way to test your market and adjust your plans with confidence.

Tips for Success

- **Offer small bonuses:**
    - Signed copies, digital wallpapers, or behind-the-scenes sketches.
- **Set clear timelines:**
    - Tell buyers when they'll receive their comic. Transparency builds trust.
- **Promote consistently:**
    - Post reminders during the pre-order window.
- **Keep communication open:**
    - Share updates on progress to reassure buyers.

How To Properly Launch Your First Comic

Launching your first comic is not just about announcing a release date. It is about bringing people along for the journey, so they feel invested long before the book is finished. The more your audience sees the process, the more connected they feel to the final product.
Below are simple, effective ways to build excitement and momentum as you move toward launch day.

Share Your Progress

People love seeing the creative process. It makes them feel like insiders. Share moments like:

- The sketching process with music in the background
- Character concepts, notes, and even corrections or mistakes

- Page and panel breakdowns to show how the story takes shape
- Coloring time-lapses that reveal the transformation of a page
- Short talks about your story or theme, even if it's just you are explaining why a scene matters

The key is consistency. Post small updates regularly so your audience feels like they're walking beside you as the comic comes together.

Create Teasers

Teasers spark curiosity without giving too much away. Think of them as breadcrumbs leading people toward your launch. Share things like:

- Snippets of the cover art
- Quick character videos or animated sketches
- Random finished pages or panels
- Progress shots showing how close you are to completion
- Keep it short and intriguing. Teasers should make people say, "***I want to see more.***"

Share Strategically, Not Stressfully

When you're just starting out, it's tempting to share everything about your comic the moment excitement strikes. However, revealing too much too soon can create pressure, set expectations you're not prepared to meet, or lock you into details that may still change. I've learned that keeping some aspects private until they're fully developed makes the entire process smoother and far less stressful.

Share just enough to spark interest while protecting your timeline—and your peace of mind.

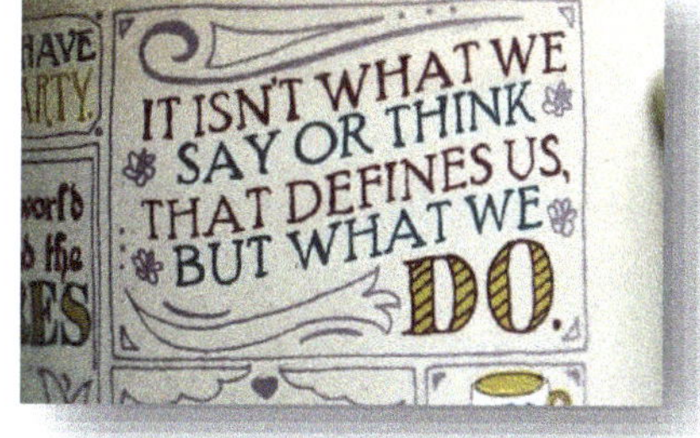

Create Sales Funnels

Building hype is easier when you have a clear path that guides people from discovering your comic to eventually supporting it. A simple funnel follows four stages: **Build Awareness → Collect Emails → Nurture Your Audience → Close the Sale.**

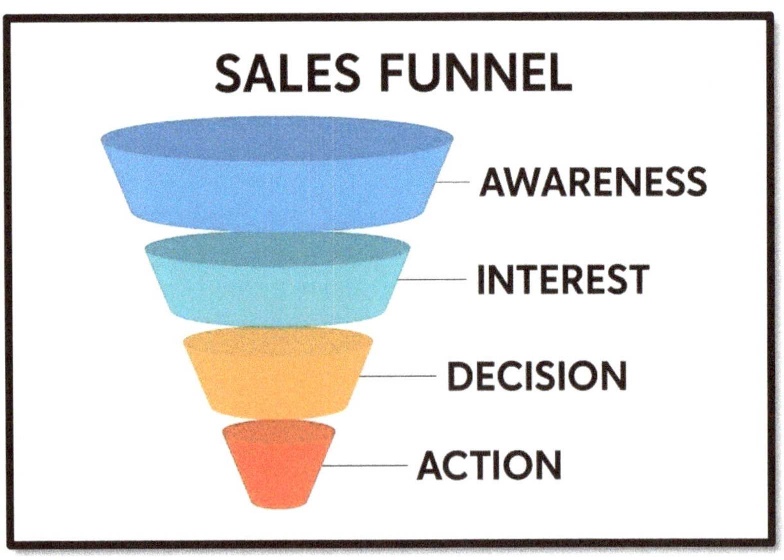

1. Build Awareness

Help people discover you and get curious about your comic.

- Share your journey, progress updates, and behind-the-scenes posts
- Post sample art, character sketches, or short teaser clips
- Join comic forums, Discord groups, and Reddit communities
- Focus on connection, not selling

2. Collect Emails

Once someone is interested, give them a place to go next.

- Use platforms like Mailchimp or MailerLite to build a mailing list
- Offer a freebie or lead magnet (sample pages, wallpapers, early looks)
- Link your sign-up form in your social media bios, posts, and stories

3. Nurture Your List and Community

Keep your audience warm, engaged, and excited.

- Run countdowns, polls, or quick interactive posts

- Respond to comments and highlight fan excitement
- Share testimonials, progress shots, and small wins

4. Close the Sale

When launch day arrives, your audience should already feel invested.

- Announce your pre-orders, crowdfunding campaign, or release
- Give clear instructions on how to support
- Remind your list why they signed up
- Make the buying process simple and direct

Before You Launch: A Mindset Shift

Most creators are far more comfortable making their comic than talking about it. Sharing progress, building excitement, and guiding people toward a launch can feel awkward or unnatural at first. That discomfort is normal. Promotion is not about becoming a salesperson. It is about learning to communicate your enthusiasm in a way that feels honest and manageable. When you treat your launch as an extension of your creative process rather than a performance, everything becomes easier. Your goal is simply to invite people along for the journey.

Chapter 5 — Launch Mindset Checklist

What you should feel prepared to do before releasing your comic:

1. ☐ I understand how to share my progress in a natural way.
2. ☐ I know how to build excitement without feeling salesy.
3. ☐ I feel comfortable talking about my journey and creative process.
4. ☐ I understand how to prepare my audience for launch.
5. ☐ I know how to create teasers that spark curiosity.
6. ☐ I feel confident choosing a launch approach that fits my personality.

Chapter 6 – Publishing Made Simple

Publishing is the moment your comic goes from files on your computer to something readers can actually hold or download. Here's how to prepare and launch with confidence.

Step 1 – Prepare Your Files

For Print (PDFs):

- Export all pages at high quality (300 DPI is standard).
- Merge them into one single PDF in the correct order.
- Double-check trim size, bleed, and margins so nothing important gets cut off.

For Digital (eBooks/Webcomics):

- Use **RGB color** (better for screens).
- No bleed needed.
- Export in formats your platform supports:
    - **PDF** (most common)
    - **ePub** (for eBook stores)
    - **PNG/JPG sequence** (for Webtoon, Tapas, or similar platforms)

Step 2 – Covers

Your cover is the first thing readers see, so make sure it's set up correctly.

- Use the template provided by your chosen platform (Amazon KDP, IngramSpark, Lulu, Mixam).
- Keep the spine and barcode areas clear.
- Convert your ISBN into a barcode. Most POD platforms provide free ones, or you can generate your own.
- Save the cover as a **separate PDF**.

Step 3 – Acquire Proofs

Proofs are your safety net — they catch mistakes before readers do.

- **Digital Proofs**: Platforms give you a preview to check page order, margins, and cover alignment.
- **Physical Proofs**: Always order at least one copy before going live. This step is critical for spotting color issues, text errors, or layout problems.
    - Amazon proofs are the fastest and cheapest, but they come watermarked as "*not for resale.*"

Step 4 – Upload & Publish

Now it's time to go live:

- Upload your interior PDF and cover file.
- Fill in metadata: title, description, ISBN (if needed), and keywords.
- Set pricing:
    - Cover your costs.
    - Stay competitive with similar comics.
    - Price digital editions lower than print.
- Approve the proof, then hit **Publish!**

Congratulations – You've taken your idea From Pitch to Publish!

You've taken your idea all the way from concept to completion. Step by step, you've now walked through the entire process of:

- Turning an idea into a comic.
- Building pages and preparing file
- Marketing and community engagement
- Publishing with various platforms and distributors

What may have felt overwhelming at first has now become a clear, repeatable process. That you can take with you wherever you go.

You don't need to be a professional artist or have a big budget; you've proven that persistence, a solid workflow, and the courage to share your story are enough to bring a comic into the world.

Key Lessons to Carry Forward

- **Progress beats perfection.** Every step taken, no matter how small, is a victory.
- **Systems matter.** Checklists, templates, and workflows are your allies. They help you stay stead and consistent on the days when nothing else does
- **Community is key.** Share your journey, connect with readers, and let your audience grow alongside you.

By pressing publish, you are not just releasing a book. You are claiming your place among creators who turned imagination into something real. Publishing is proof that your ideas matter, and your comic doesn't have to be flawless to deserve a place in the world.

So don't stall. Export your files, set a fair price, order your proof, and press publish. The moment you do, you'll not only join the growing community of independent creators, but you'll also prove to yourself that you can finish what you started. That's the moment you became a published creator, and that's an achievement that will stay with you forever.

Word From the Author

Thank you for taking the time to read this book and absorb its lessons. When I first started creating comics, I wished there had been a guide that spoke directly to beginners and offered clear, honest, and practical advice on what to do next. That is the guide I set out to create for you.

If this book has helped you gain clarity, confidence, or momentum, then it has accomplished exactly what I intended. I plan to continue creating, teaching, and building resources that support new and growing creators. This is only the beginning.

Stay tuned for what comes next, because your journey has just started, and I'm honored to be a part of it.

Glossary

Beat Sheet

A beat sheet is a simple outline that lists the major moments of your story in order. It helps you understand your narrative structure at a glance, so you always know where your characters are headed and what emotional or plot beats come next.

Bleed

Bleed is the extra space around your artwork that extends beyond the final trim size. It ensures that when the printer cuts the pages, your backgrounds and full-page art reach the edge cleanly without leaving unintended white borders.

Caption

A caption is a text box used for narration or internal thoughts that don't belong in a speech balloon. Captions help guide the reader through time jumps, scene changes, or character reflections.

Character Arc

A character arc is the internal journey a character goes through from the beginning of the story to the end. It reflects how they grow, change, or learn as the plot unfolds.

Climax

The climax is the most intense, high-stakes moment of your story where the central conflict reaches its peak. It's the point where your character must make a decisive choice or face the biggest challenge.

Dialogue

Dialogue is the spoken text between characters, usually placed inside speech balloons. It reveals personality, moves the story forward, and shapes how readers connect with your cast.

EPUB

EPUB is a digital book format required by platforms like Kindle and Apple Books. It preserves your page layout and ensures your comic displays correctly across different devices.

Flats

Flats are the first stage of coloring where you fill in solid base colors for characters, objects, and backgrounds. They act as a guide for adding shading, highlights, and effects later.

Gutter

The gutter is the space between panels or the inner fold of a printed book. Keeping important artwork and text away from the gutter prevents them from being distorted or lost during binding.

Inking

Inking is the process of refining your rough sketches into clean, final linework. It defines shapes, adds clarity, and prepares your page for coloring.

ISBN

An ISBN is a unique identification number assigned to your book so bookstores, libraries, and distributors can track and catalog it. Each format of your comic—digital, paperback, hardcover—requires its own ISBN.

Lettering

Lettering is the process of adding dialogue, captions, sound effects, and text to your comic. Good lettering improves readability, guides the reader's eye, and enhances the emotional tone of each scene.

Metadata

Metadata is the descriptive information about your book—such as title, description, keywords, and categories—that helps online platforms understand and recommend it. Strong metadata improves discoverability.

Midpoint

The midpoint is a major turning point in your story where something significant shifts. It raises the stakes, reveals new information, or changes your character's direction.

Panel

A panel is a single frame that captures one moment in your story. The size, shape, and arrangement of panels control pacing and guide how readers experience the narrative.

Print-On-Demand (POD)

Print-on-demand is a publishing method where books are printed only when someone orders them. It eliminates the need for large print runs and reduces upfront costs for creators.

Proof Copy

A proof copy is a test print of your comic that allows you to check colors, margins, text placement, and overall quality before approving the final version. It's your chance to catch issues that aren't visible on a screen.

Safe Zone

The safe zone is the inner area of your page where all important text and artwork must stay to avoid being cut off during trimming. Staying inside the safe zone ensures a clean, professional final print.

Script

A comic script is the written blueprint that describes each page, panel, character action, and line of dialogue. It communicates your vision clearly to artists, letterers, or your future self.

Spine

The spine is the narrow edge of your printed comic that displays the title, author name, and sometimes the publisher. Its width depends on your page count and affects how your book appears on shelves.

Thumbnail

A thumbnail is a small, rough sketch used to plan page layouts and panel flow before creating full-size artwork. Thumbnails help you experiment quickly with pacing and composition.

Trim Size

Trim size is the final width and height of your printed comic after it's cut down from the larger printing sheet. Choosing the right trim size affects your layout, printing cost, and how your comic feels in the reader's hands.

Turning Point

A turning point is a moment in your story where something shifts—emotionally, narratively, or structurally. It pushes the plot forward and forces your character to react or change.

Resources

This section gathers the tools, platforms, and services mentioned throughout the book so you have an easy place to return to whenever you need support. Everything listed here is beginner-friendly, widely used, and reliable for comic creators at any stage.

Writing & Planning Tools

These tools help you outline, script, and organize your ideas.

- **Google Docs** – Free, cloud-based writing tool great for scripts and collaboration.
- **LibreOffice** – Free offline writing suite for drafting and formatting documents.
- **Adobe Acrobat / PDF Gear** – Useful for combining pages, exporting PDFs, and reviewing final files.

Drawing Tablets

Reliable options for digital art at different price points.

- **Wacom Intuos** – Affordable, durable, and ideal for beginners.
- **XP-Pen Tablets** – Great mid-range tablets with screen and non-screen models.

- **iPad + Apple Pencil** – Portable and powerful, widely used for full comic production.

Drawing & Art Software

Free Options

- **Krita** – Full-featured digital painting program with layers and brushes.
- **MediBang Paint** – Manga-focused tools, cloud saving, and built-in comic features.
- **FireAlpaca** – Lightweight and beginner-friendly for clean comic pages.

Paid Options

- **Clip Studio Paint (Pro/EX)** – Industry standard for comics and manga with panel tools, 3D models, and lettering features.
- **Procreate** – Fast, intuitive iPad app great for sketching, inking, and full pages.
- **Adobe Photoshop** – Professional art software with powerful editing tools.

Publishing Platforms

Digital Publishing

- **Amazon KDP** – Largest digital marketplace with global reach.

- **Gumroad** – Ideal for direct-to-reader digital sales.
- **Apple Books** – Popular platform for digital comics.
- **Your Own Website** – Full control over pricing, branding, and customer experience.

Print-On-Demand (POD)

- **Amazon KDP** – Fast fulfillment and global availability.
- **Barnes & Noble Press** – Access to B&N's online store and potential in-store placement.
- **IngramSpark** – Wide bookstore and library distribution with high print quality.
- **Lulu** – High-quality printing and integration with Shopify and WooCommerce.

ISBN & Barcode Tools

- **Bowker** – Official ISBN provider in the United States.
- **Kindlepreneur Barcode Generator** – Free, clean barcode creation.

- **TEC-IT Barcode Generator** – Free barcode generator for print-ready files.

Crowdfunding Platforms

- **Kickstarter** – Most popular platform for comic campaigns.
- **Indiegogo** – Flexible funding options and extended campaign tools.

Artist-Finding Platforms

- **Behance** – Professional portfolios with many comic and manga artists.
- **Fiverr** – Wide range of artists offering commissions.
- **Upwork —** Freelance marketplace where artists often advertise commissions.

www.ingramcontent.com/pod-product-compliance
Ingram Content Group UK Ltd.
Pitfield, Milton Keynes, MK11 3LW, UK
UKHW061132310726
14090UKWH00035B/706